Awake at Dawn

For Nani Ammi and Nanu Deda

On Gathering Flowers: An Introduction to Awake at Dawn By Kavita N. Ramdas

There comes a time when elders turn to the young, not just for strength and hope, but for their wisdom. When our complacency and collaboration with the status quo slips into silence and complicity. If we are very fortunate, in those moments, bursting upon us with all the force of nature – a tufaan, a sandstorm, a volcano, perhaps – the young rise up. As if from the earth herself they rise. When they do, we are forced to stop in our tracks. Like the monsoons they are a force unchecked - they flood us with feelings we had tamed, tamped down, hushed into obedience, and locked up. They sweep past our objections, our assumptions, and wash away years of concealed power. When the downpour is over, we realize they have revealed tiny tender possibilities.

We are living in such times. Students are standing in peaceful, non-violent, conscientious resistance to genocide and apartheid. The elders, the ones who were supposed to hold them, water them, and nurture them have, instead, let loose the dogs of war. Across campuses, armed riot police and the National Guard have been called out to subdue and silence our kids. The educators have threatened those who most took to heart the lessons about democracy, freedom, human rights, and dignity. They face suspensions and expulsions. The media call them a threat to peace.

The contradictions of this moment are impossible to comprehend with rational analysis. How blessed we are, therefore, to be able to turn to the wisdom, insights, and pain of an emerging young poet, Nirbhay Pratap Singh Purewal Legha, for solidarity and solace. A student of physics, and untrained in any formal sense in this field, his writings sharply capture our tortured historical context. A few of them will take your breath away with their delicate unraveling of privilege, profit, people, and planet. The poet's selection is a prickly reminder of the reality within which we have raised his generation. In Paradise Lost, he voices the despair of living with extinction as the closest companion. In other poems, like Punj Aab and TSA Abuse, we catch the sense of loss in the lives of migrants, of the otherness of black and brown bodies no matter where they find themselves. Here too are struggles of living with anxiety, insecurity, and the burrowing creatures that will not let us rest, for they are our own beloved pets/pests – familiar not only to a teenager or young adult but to us elders, right now, right here.

Yet, across the collection, echoes of hope persist as our hearts are drawn into the eerie blossoms in the Antarctic, wild mustard in the spring, sea glass on a beach - images that are made even more vivid with the pen sketches accompanying each poem. Even as we journey with wanna-be superheroes to conquer Mars or the moon, Legha's poems always return us to the Earth. No matter how fragile and threatened all of us are, we are also persistently, absurdly resilient. We grow roots and stretch out toward the sun, even on the edge of a precipice, hoping to be gathered. For all our sakes, I am so pleased that Purewal Legha has the gumption and generosity to share this bunch of wildflowers with the world.

420 and More

There are parts of me I wish I could let go

A gnawing, scratching ferret burrowed deep within my

soul

The more I feel it, the deeper it goes

The more I want it out, the bigger it grows

My mind grows around it, entrapping it within a cage

Unintentional, yet made by me, all the same,

It carries with it, claws of shame

They scratch through my self-respect, my honor, my

pride in my name

When it was young I let it in

I was innocent, curious, naive you might say

Now I'm a bit older, I've seen its ways

I've tried and tried, but it won't leave through the same

gates

That ferret's a part of me now

No escaping that truth, try though I might

 It's not leaving the back of my mind

These parts of me I wish to let go

make me who I am and I can't let go

So I'll do what I can and give the ferret a little hole

A place where it'll live and feed off a part of my soul

And then I'll ignore it, and I'll hope

That maybe, just maybe, it won't grow

It won't claw or scratch and it'll finally be home

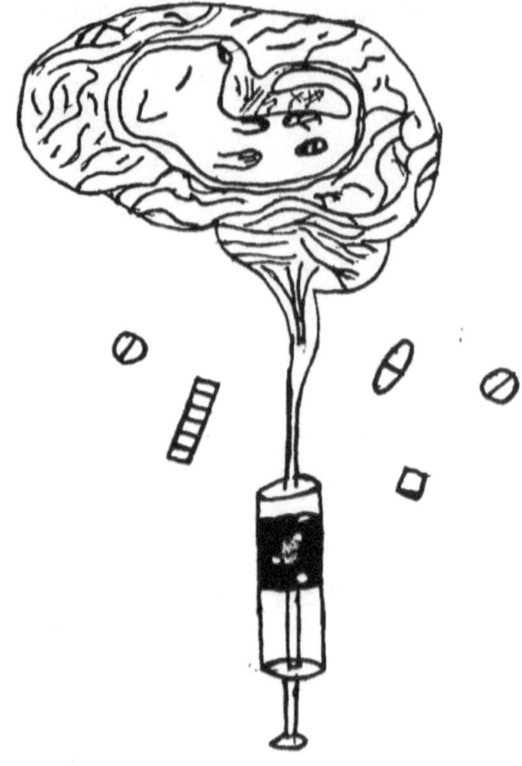

Red, White, and Blue

Blue uniforms and white sheets like to see brown blood

on concrete

They hide behind hard-brimmed black caps

And slogans of protecting the world from things like

crack

Their lips spell lies of thin blue lines

Protecting "us" from shadowy hordes of "them"

A "them" they're always watching

A "them" they're stopping frisking and sometimes

robbing

Because "them" is a perpetual threat

"Them" is others that look different from "us"

Their blood belongs with dirt and dust

Policing is done by dealing with this "them"

And when "them" is not found

It is done by turning hounds loose on fellow human

beings

Waiting for fleeing or kicking and screaming

Resisting arrest, drug possession, or some form of cop

contempt done by someone who isn't white

These things can quickly be labeled as crimes

And these criminal victims so often have nothing but

fear in their eyes

Criminal is really just another word for black no better

than a slur the modern-day n-word

A word whose meaning is laced with screenings of

black-on-white fights and " airtight" cases closed within a

fortnight

Cases filled with innocent faces of young children labeled

" super predators" heartless gang-banging machines

Blue uniforms find these and pluck them from fields

filled with other black weeds

Crush them into concrete and send them off to jail "fresh

meat"

Blue uniforms aren't much different than white sheets

Both murder black skin in the street

Both punish black men for looking at pretty white bees

Both break black backs to show that the racial order is

intact

This machine works and it's always been the same

Ever since our constitution was written excluding

two-fifths of every slave

Youth's folly

We felt like an earthquake

Like we were inevitable

A shift in tectonic plates

Leaving the earth changed

We felt like comets...

Invincible...

At least till we crashed into the earth's surface

Leaving permanent scars

A mark of our purpose

We felt like waterfalls

Blasting into the land

Shifting it under our mighty torrent

Molding it with our hands

Little did we know

 We were not waterfalls

But drops of rain

...insignificant....

Deflected by a wax glaze

We were nothing thinking we were everything

But we could be everything

Enough rain can turn the ground to mush

Can delay traffic

Can crash planes

Enough rain can flood the earth

If Noah is to be trusted, then rain was once man's bane

It wiped humanities mark off the plane

Wrought havoc and killed all, till only two of each species

remained

We could be that rain

If only there were enough drops

And the land were not so vast

But perhaps, this is just youth's folly

Violence of Wine

When I was a young grape still unripe and unsure, I

clung to my vines like a sailor ashore

On an island far away and obscured

As I hit my teenage years, I grew with violence and was

fierce

My colors turned a darkish red, like a grape that's ripe

and yet

I remained unsure and my taste you couldn't endure

As I reached my plucking season, my taste was sweet and

fresh, untreated

But the farmers said to me: you're not bold, need growth,

are not complete

And right before I hit the vineyard floor, the farmer

plucked me, stripped me

Threw me in a barrel with dozens more

Left me there to work and work, till my insides did

outside burst

Tasting me from time to time, saying I'd make a bold fine

wine

He molded me as he pleased, I was trapped, found no

release

Now I'm sitting put asunder, thinking of when I'm older

Will I mature into a nice wine and work never more

Or will I work too much and sour, change my taste, and

lose my power

Will I become what I abhorred when I was still a sweet

fresh grape

With ideals and a taste for the things that make life great

Bittersweet Call

I hear the Azaan on the TV screen

The undulating call to prayer echoing

 beautiful and serene

Serene and strange

I am of a different faith

Yet, this call to prayer was meant for me

Well not for me, but rather to me

The channel I was watching wasn't religious

And this wasn't really a call to prayer

Criminal Minds or CSI, NCIS with terrorists

A man with brown skin and a thick Arabic accent

A man almost like me

That's what plays over it every time

This call is strange because it's been 19 years since 9/11

yet it still fills the air

Calling all of us terrorists

We brown men with some faith

It doesn't matter if we're Hindu, Christian, Sikh, or Jain

 to them, we are all the same

Godless enemies

Rich oil barons

Subjugators of women

Sexually assaulting people we have taken

We are named Khan, Ali, Ahmad

Followed by Al-something if we are important

Seen wearing a turban, shemagh, or bedouin shalwar

Planting bombs or crashing train cars

That call emits a subconscious signal to be afraid

A subconscious signal for them but for me a bittersweet

taste

The sweetness that comes with unity

With sympathy

With the oneness that only bitter can produce

This bitter

This othering

This American pus

Oozing from a pimple filled with racism

With fear and disgust

To be loathed can lead to love

And so this Azaan plays

And I think of all the people that feel hate

And I feel love

Love for all my Muslim brethren who felt the same hate

Love for all other brown men targeted for looking like

men of that faith

Love for those who hate

Because they're still grieving

But also anger and rage

Because their grieving shouldn't be keeping so many

others so far away

And instead of praying I curse 9/11

I curse that blood-soaked day

Nation's Lost

Learned men talk of the news

What's happening away from their views

The things they don't need to see

Because they've got their degrees

The rockets launched by a group

The marching of military boots

But not the bodies lying in the mosque

Hush Hush

Their voices cry

 If we speak too loud They'll pass us by

So we quietly whisper

I don't think it was justified

There are too many children trapped inside

How long has this been going on

Why do they talk only to decry the violence of one side

Hush Hush

You're being too loud the learned men say

The cameras will go away

Our shackles are rattling, roaring now we wonder how

long will they drown them out

The stones children throw have prayers written within

But no learned men seem to have read the prayers or seen

sin

HUSH HUSH

No

These learned men talk

And they talk so loud that we fear the world won't be

able to hear the planes and bombs

Won't hear the cries of a mother losing their child

Won't hear the howling kids who've lost limbs

Won't hear the silence

The silence that screams loudest of all

The silence of a people killed off

A nation lost

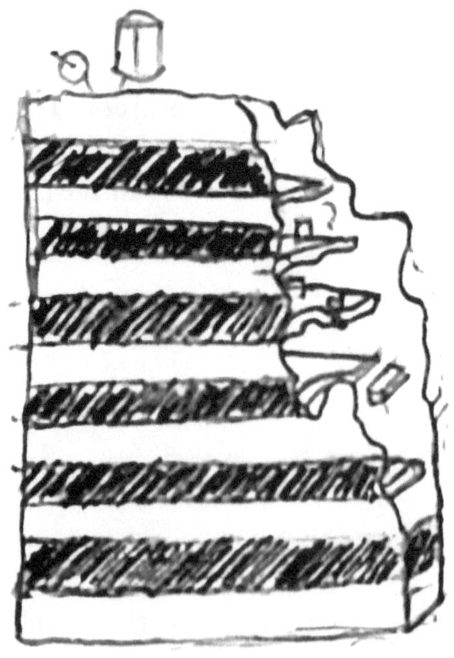

The Moon and Mars

We still look to the stars for the things we've lost

The things we've squandered

Clear skies and clean water

We used to look at the moon and think

That maybe it held lost boons

The holy grail, some heroes' chain mail

The love we lost, the memories we left behind

Now we know better...

We've seen our gray servant's surface

We found no secrets hidden in its mines

We're more rational without magical thinking

We're self-assured, not God-fearing

But still, we dream of a mystical land called Mars

Maybe if we terraform Mars

The stars could hold another home of ours

If we build another atmosphere

We can move there instead of staying here

You see, we've torn a couple of holes in ours

We can build forests from scratch

And rivers and dams

And we won't have to deal with the floods

Or feel the heat that comes

With a planet packed to the brim with carbon fumes

Some of ours decided that they don't want to fight it

That our planet's lost forever and they'll be the ones to

find it

Once more sitting on the barren rock of Mars

Tony Stark

I'm done waiting on superheroes

Because Superman's dead

He's left for Krypton

Left from my head

I'm done waiting for someone to save me

Because nowadays saviors say "pay me"

The seed that was planted when I was younger

The seed that said I could be unique

Something special, something super

Is dead

I stopped watering it, and its life fled

I stopped waiting on Iron Man when Elon Musk came

into play

I stopped waiting when I realized that Bezos and Bill

Gates

Each got their powers the same way

Colonizing interactions

For gain there is pain

Nothing is for free

So few of us reap the rewards we were told were our

destiny

We grow old and if we work hard in the right job then

maybe we might have enough

But even if we become lawyers and doctors

We won't have superpowers

Our freedom is constrained by our working-class gains

Modern-day superheroes don't wear capes

They have multimillion-dollar planes

They have huge houses in every country

And do whatever fits their fancy

Because no one has the power to stop them

They really aren't heroes

Of them being super there is no doubt

But heroes I can't give them they care not for us louts

They care about their power and owning everything we

call ours

Our time and bodies but also more

Our search history our private thoughts

Our chats with family

 Our grocery deliveries

Are all theirs for sale

I'll never be a superhero

I've consigned myself to this fate

Being super can only be done on the corpses of slaves

Internet Hymn

I took my phone up off my bed and sent a silent prayer to

the god of internet

A video for the whole world and no one at once

I spoke in an elevated tone the form of every similar

prayer a high energy bursting forth into the air

Creating something from nothing a silent public

devotion an art piece

A performance for a crowd to which I expose my sins, my

hopes my fears my dreams

A crowd that knows both everything and nothing

Not one person on the internet on God's great web

knows what I'm like in real life

But everyone knows who and what I am

I am nothing to them but they are my everything

I am nothing before this god a mere ant but to me this

god is everything

I am it and it is me this is my algorithm it changes to my

whims but still makes me

Shapes my thoughts and transforms my very soul till I am

no more me but something new and unknown

Radicalized and funneled into a pre-existing mould

I am changed by it yet it does my bidding a god of

trickery lying, waiting

For the next scrap of data

The next piece to convert

Till all I am is a product

This great god of Internet will never love me as I love it

All it can do is take take take

It demands from me my energy, my time and gives

nothing but cognitive decline

Oh this god is a cruel god and one day

I'll cut off its hand and walk away

Walk into a new sun into a fresh day

Go out touch grass smell flowers and pray

To a different god one who gives one who is

The truth this god has hidden away

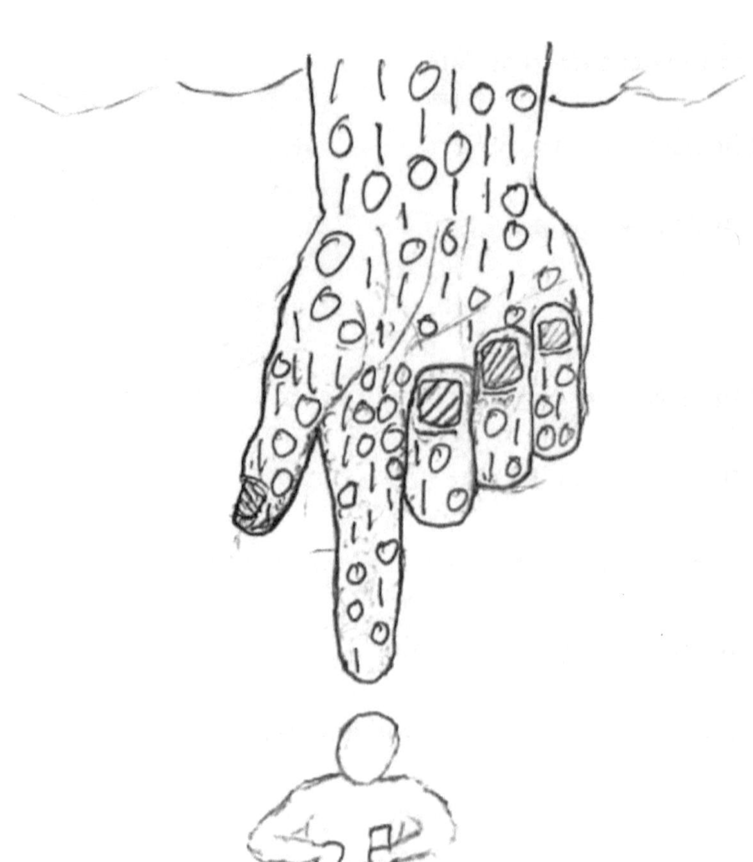

Parking lot berries

A walk after lunch with my work friends turned magical

We were transported to ancient forests

Using an app to connect to our ancestors' knowledge we

divined the edible from the raw or rotten

We plucked these hard seeds from an invasive European

species

Strawberry trees

We filled our hands pockets and mouths in a field of
asphalt filled with metal cows

Paradise Lost

Roughly eighty-four years ago

Science could prove that the earth was burning in our

energy refuse

The generations before me knew

Chevron too knew the truth

The greed of our parents ignited the fuel

But what should I know?

I'm just a child

It matters not that everything is changing

That this earth that is burning the earth where I'll be

living

I'm not old enough to be taken seriously

but I must bear the weight of the ending of everything

I've ever known

And accept that everyone after me will never know

The paradise traded in for gold

Teenage problems now include the end of their world

Wisdom seeps from their fear-scarred brains

Listen hear their anguish

The younger you and them are not the same

Anthropocene

We beat the earth into submission

We conquered every species

Touched every inch

But this earth we've defeated

Is where we're trapped

There is no escape

And we can't fix this mess we've made

This was our will

And the will of all those before

Those who polluted fully informed

Neglected their projections for profit

And turned a blind eye to the misery they caused

But what was is now gone

Now we are all in the same boat

Facing a rising wall of water

Made of glaciers older than us

Conquered with our black gold

Still, we deny our role

Countless species have gone extinct

And the seas no longer hold fish

But this was all nature, right?

The climate crisis doesn't exist!

We can deny all we want, but the truth is

The tides are coming

Any day now

Coming

To wash all the skyscrapers

Coming

To destroy everything we ever built

With that oily black money

Coming

The profit made will soon be for nothing

The tides are coming

This crisis won't last

And like a virus that made its host breathe its last

We'll have nowhere to go

Nowhere to call home

As the pyre burns us with the body

Flowers in Antarctica

There's Flowers blooming in Antarctica

Yellow and Green Create Carpets and Weave over the icy

slopes

These Beautiful Bushes pushing snow creating an

undergrowth

The seeds of a forest that once was and may once more

grow

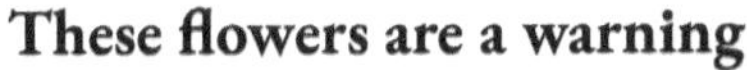

These flowers are a warning

An Ancient tablet preparing for a Tsunami

The stones in a river that read caution hunger is coming,

"If you see me weep"

These flowers should be terrifying

Like God's face, it is something we shouldn't see

The light that would blind us turn us to salt

stone and wither us down to bones is shining

bursting forth from snow

And Those who warned us look not into it for it is

brighter than the sun are locked up their words hidden

their lives undone

The ice that kept back these delicate cancerous growths

has melted

The Earth has warmed back to before humans existed

Viruses, bacteria, and other once-frozen menaces have

pushed forth from permafrost

Riding our climate crisis' horse they have come our souls

to reap

Weep for the signs are here

See the divine face and let loose tears

But humans just like flowers are resilient

When the frost grows over us we will wait, be patient

Once our towers have tumbled

Our hierarchies crumbled

We will be free to grow like flowers in a desolate frozen

land

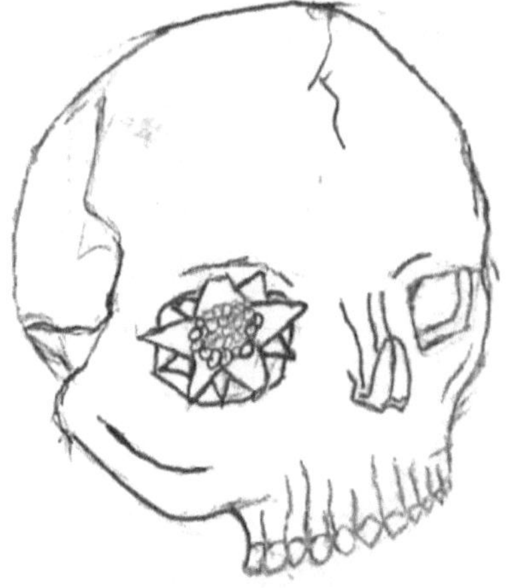

Dying Ocean

Far beneath the cerulean blue

Lies a different view than what I'd imagined

A view empty but not quite

But not quite brimming with life

A view filled with space

So much space

An empty nothingness different from the visions of the

sea Nat Geo promised to me

A few sparse schools with nothing to do

The corals they lived in had died

Hunks of trash

Water bottles, and plastic bags

A fishnet lost some time ago

Wrapping around the skeletons of scallops and yellowfin

Starved to death

Half rotting with scales slipping, and eyes falling

Netting together until it grew to the size of a wrecking

ball

And there I stood below it

On a dessert made of the same rocks that stood towering

above

Puncturing empty grey skies

Empty except for the netting

A cloud of garbage and bones inviting more of the few

fish left to their death

A cloud that grew with time as I stood paralyzed

A cloud that swept up other nets

Deathtraps cast by fishers, and quietly forgotten

Ballooning to the size of Texas

Absorbing all life

It grew and grew

And it's growing to this day

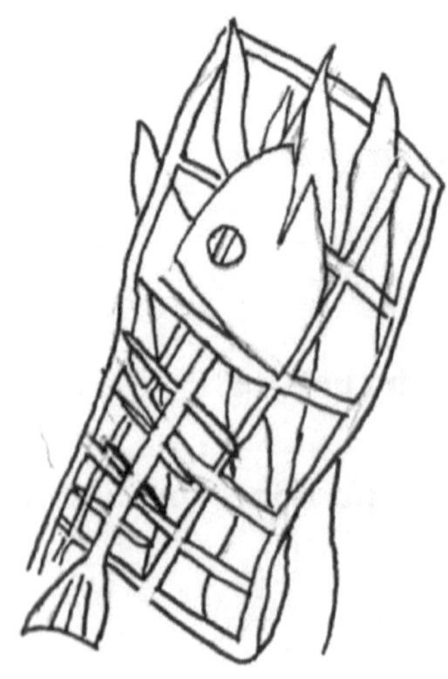

Colonized people

They preserved the savage idol in a cage made of glass

Out of reach of worshipers mocking them from its stance

They took his legs and cut his hands to make a

square-shaped man

They displayed their culture's finest men birthed from

hammers and stone

They tore the paint away because ancient art should be

done in white not blue or gold

Slowly they rewrote the books from which our children

learned

Till all that's left of Athens is ruins and Indian heritage

contains British railroads

These our heroes our saviors whose burden is far too

much for any man alone

These men once white have now been tanned a darker

tone

They've kept up the destruction of history in the name of

something old

Broke down the ancient masjid for a mandir of which

stories were once told

These our colonizers stole the deva's hands and feet

These our colonizers changed the Indian heartbeat

Punj Aab

I was walking through wild mustard in the Spring

Thinking of who I am and who I was raised to be

Of the *saag* and *makki di roti* my parents fed me

And of the language, they taught me

The language that leaves my tongue in a broken cart

which creaks and squeaks and has spots of rot

The culture that I forgot

Those spots of fungi that up and grew from the blood I

shed of the lamb whose head I swept because to it I was

always foreign never a friend, and too self-important

I'm thinking of fitting in, of the caution tape I'm covered

in

the neon sign flashing above my eyes every time I sit

inside a room of people with different ancestral ties

And setting off to the skies

Being met with hostile eyes

A stranger

Always a danger

And of the fruits of my sacrifice, the price of blood I paid

for a chance to not be foreign

Of that lamb's pain and the desert that it left me in

Of trying and trying to claw my way back, hoping the

lamb's head would reattach

Then I'd be free to be at last somewhere where people

might see me as just a man, not a turban or complex

oddity

 Just an odd man, an innocent, a student, and most

importantly, a human

TSA abuse

Those who've seen my unshorn hair number very few

My blood, my family, those who've known me since after

I left the womb

And two TSA agents who moved me to a backroom

They told me to remove an article of my identity

And had me place it in a bin which usually contains shoes

They did not give me a reason

I asked them many times

Is there anything I can do?

Is it the three cups of coffee I consumed?

What might have caused this?

Why was the machine focused on this symbol of my

religious views?

Can *I* pat it down?

That's what they let me do every other time I fly

I know that my hands are clean

That there's nothing in my bag but poetry and school

things

And nothing on my head but a symbol that says I'm free

Except I'm not right now

I've been detained without charge

I'd much rather they had me strip naked and cough than

remove these six yards

As they shuffle me along

My legs go limp, and my hands begin to shake

I've never felt this before

Nausea mixing in my stomach with righteous

indignation, humiliation, and hate

At a system that is perverse

To the point of making a nineteen-year-old student

remove something he holds dearer than his life for some

false security

A system that has no respect for this article

That treats it like a jacket, laptop, or belt

A system that doesn't even protect what it claims to

With a failure rate of ninety-seven percent

But I was red-flagged for the audacity to try and board

While looking un-western

While looking a little different

That's probably the tester they caught

The three percent missing from a complete fail track

record

This security theatre serves only as a play for the little

white lady in the back

Who was eyeing suspiciously the brown man in a "hat"

Staring at my bag

Thinking of Bush, Bin Laden, and Iraq

One of the men proceeds to walk up and pat down my

hair no care for my personal space

The obvious emptiness in it stared us both in the face

No one had violated me in this way

No one had so simply conveyed the irregularity my

receded hairline posed to this nation's ethos

The other came back and I proceeded to retie my turban

With the door left slightly open

So that just a few more people might be offered a peek

With this humiliation complete

I recovered my bag and my shoes

Allowed to board my plane

Still shaking with rage

But still full of conviction in my faith

Knowing that even knowing everything humans will still

make mistakes

Knowing that true faith is something no harassment

could ever shake

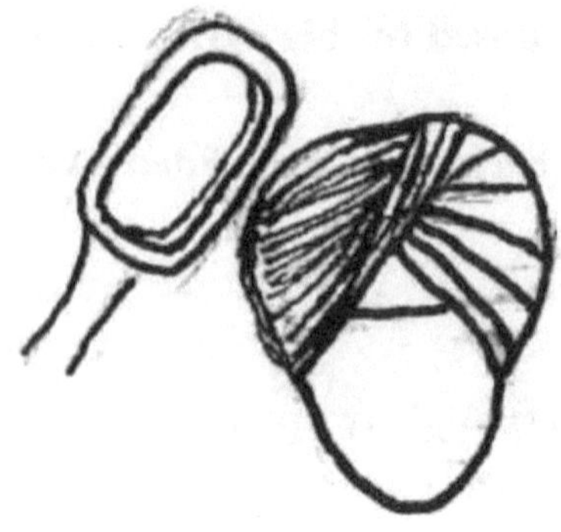

Banjara

I wish I were a traveler

But not the kind that exists on this earth

If I were a traveler,

I would chase the sweet whispers of the wind

Follow the sparks it ignites in my heart and my mind till

I reach their end

If I were a traveler I would move quick

I would leave just after tasting a comfortable routine's

sweet kiss

Chasing roses, not dimes

Finding knowledge where it hides

Looking in caves for something that might fill the one in

the center of my life

I would be free to explore, not shackled to the floor that

society gave me

Not shackled to my grades, my money, or my race

The things, others decided meant everything

I could be a mind, free from my body

A wisp of sand in a sandstorm, a drop of water in the eye

of a hurricane

A wandering soul

Working on whatever fits my fancy

But this Iron chain won't break

Not so easily

It's grown around me gradually and eventually, maybe It

might consume me

Another number amongst the hordes

A faceless worker, a product, and producer

Now while it holds me, while I see this bleak gray future

laid before me

All I can do is chisel away, working through its metallic

gray, and satisfy my curiosity with stories

Black Hole

The stars interact

Sending sprays, beams of light

Sometimes white

Other times blue, green, red, and purple

But I'm black

A star that punctured the plane

A black hole in conversational space

Invisible, absorbing all the words they say

I'm stuck listening, but I can't contribute

This light of mine is sealed away

Trapped inside my confines

Swirling in warped space

These stars around me, clearly they don't want me

If they did, they wouldn't have let me explode

They would have shared in all my light's glory

When I was big, red, and old

But instead, they left me for dead

And I began to blend

In with the rest of their domain

This party zooms around me, expanding in different

ways

Space stretches and contracts

Stars leave the intergalactic pact

Creating clusters with their centers, set in different ways

But I stay

A black slate

A person or at least person-shaped

With light, bright emotions building at unseen rates

Absorbing with information forming

Breaking contorting

Sculpting things with light sent from that other plane

An alien figure

A weird creature

Out of nowhere, a wisp may escape

From my strange distorted cave

A piece of radiation

You'll miss it if you aren't listening

But if you hear it, it might burn through your brain

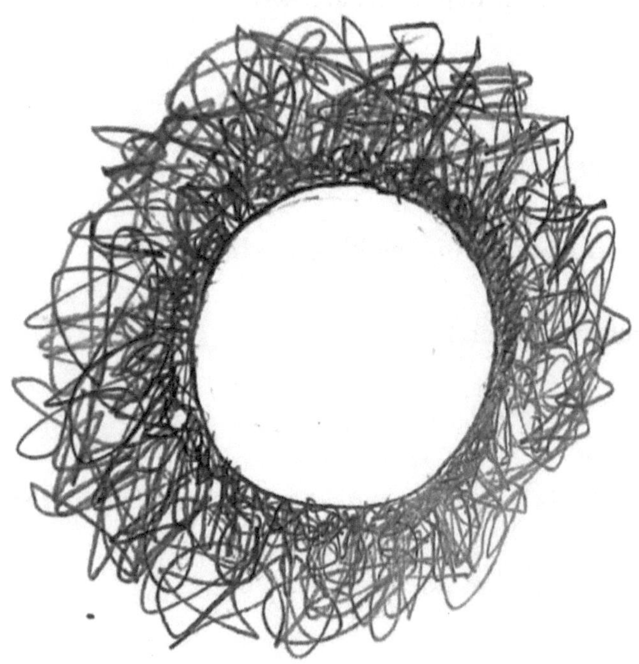

To my Anxieties

Your hair is like a lion's mane, bold and confident

Waving in the wind

Waving my confidence, my self-assurance

Your skin is sandstone, strong and thick

It rubs through mine, making it a little softer

Weaker, with each flick

Your voice is bold it drowns out my own it's why I speak

so softly when I'm not alone

You're always so playful, so strong, so secure

You pick at my brain all day and night

With those long slender needles of yours

You wake me at odd hours in the night whispering sickly

sweet words of fear, a durian fruit you've grown in my

ear

You leech off me

Without my fears, it seems you couldn't survive

But without you, neither could I

We're connected, the two of us

As if fate has woven us together, our perfect

imperfection, forever dotted across the night sky

Our umbilical cord tethers us together like mother and

child

just as you feed off me, your blood drips deep into mine

But the same fate that tethered us has destined one of us

to die

If I lose you on my journey through life, I will grow with

skin like Iron

A voice like a lion, and the confidence of a burning star

But for now, you are mine

Consumed or consuming, you are changing your food

supply

G itti

I wrote a piece of Graffiti

Carved my name into a bench

I hoped that whoever sat there would see it and wonder

Who had desecrated their place of rest

I hoped that they might see it so they could hear me

Shouting from the top of my lungs:

Look at me!

Do you see me?!

I will not be Ignored!

I hoped that they might wonder, if only for a second or

two,

Revolted at my vandalization of their calming refuge

Who was this person?

Why did they do what they did?

When were they here?

How did they live?

If they saw and wondered

Maybe I'd live forever

Wading into the minds of every weary traveler who

starred and still tried to ignore me

Tried to ignore

My voice

My scream

Shimmering Beach

There's a glass beach in Mendocino

Sea glass pebbles cover the California coast

Taillights and industrial waste from another generation

A revolting putrid trash pile turned to the ocean's

gemstones

It lives at the end of an unassuming field

Bursting with indigenous flowers and fat gray squirrels

unfazed by human contact

It breathes the glass it's made of

Gaining and losing matter to the beat of the tides

I came one day like a Viking pirate

Sailing concrete oceans in a Ford

I stole its breath away, filled my pockets with sea glass

Plundered its hallowed shores

I took them to keep in a little wooden box

 Tokens of the sea, its jewelry

A glistening sparkling dragon's horde left on a beach

But the few closest to me will always be the seven pieces I

took at a beach right by me

When I went hunting for hours

Little emeralds I dug out of a sandy mountain

Gems studding the hilt of a crooked wooden

spoon I carved

An Ugly Question

There was a mouse in my house

It crept in through my foundation

A silent infestation

Something I couldn't seem to get out of my head

No matter how many traps, how many sticky vats

How many poison corks with spring swords and yellow

cheese I set

I couldn't lead it to its death

An earworm

An Idea that's crawled in, that's made me a man possessed

A question harkening me to bury myself in stacks of

books and wonder in little nooks, till finally, I know it

An enigmatic abrasion that's burst through the

floorboards of my brain

A furry grimy creature crawling on all fours

Dragging its paws on my kitchen floors

Leaving scritch-scratches and fleas

Scuffing me up making my head buzz as it creeps

Moving slowly towards my bed, the place I control, the

core of my home where I feel safe, secure, and alone.

This ugly little rat with sticky brown hair, gnarled teeth,

and breath like garbage burning with rotten flesh, made

its way into my sacred hole

A grotesque monstrosity that began to gloat

As I stared at the gashes in its matted coat

Saying that I would never understand it, never see its

reality

And slowly it struck me

I stared just long enough to find something,

The answer

The proof

A truth obscured in the appearance of a rat

It shifted its bones and let out soft sweet purrs

Changed back from a rodent to a cat

Set itself down next to my crown snuggling and licking

me ever so softly as I crept into a peaceful rest

Breathless Dream

I had a dream

God set me free

He let me forget about gravity

I could fly above the mountains and soar above the sea

I was filled with joy

I was gay and felt unadulterated glee

Up, up, and away I flew

The whole earth I could see

He let me play with Jupiter, Mars, and all the stars from

other galaxies

I was ecstatic

All was mine

No, all was me

Then I panicked, felt dizzy and frantic

I realized I couldn't breathe

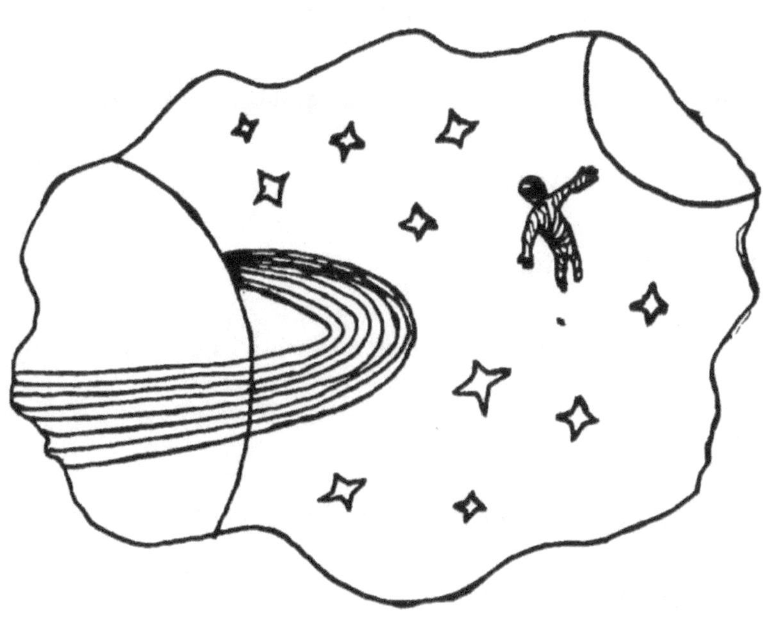

Morning Hike

The trees, the birds, the smell of the earth

The red-browns, greens, purples, and whites

Inspiration at every turn

The moss on trees, the flowers, the leaves

Swirling red marks like Jupiter's bark

The fog obscuring, lions-a-lurking, hares running,

bolting deep into the pines

Poems are forming

They're growing, then falling and blowing off the windy

mountainside

Writing on trees and saving the leaves before they blow

away out of my mind

Historic Currents

This is the sea...

Its vastness beyond comprehension

Its depth cannot be perceived

The ashes of my ancestors flow through it and it flows to

me

One day soon *I'll* flow through it

Lost, in a never-ending reverie

It'll carry me to a distant land, and then to my offspring

yet to be

Lotus Roots

We're taught to fear tears

But they grow like flowers

Despite our ego's powers

Into a beautiful bouquet of truths

So beautiful it needs to be viewed

To be seen to be felt to be touched and smelled

But they've asked me to lock it inside

To let it wither and die and they've taught me to

objectify

To care not for true beauty

But to view things with lustful eyes

To take what I want without a thought for who what or

why

We're told our feelings

Are leeching creeping vines

Infecting our masculine side

And poems, feelings personified

Are vilified

My first reaction to poetry in class

Was that I would rather rebar be driven

From my eyeballs to the start of my spine

Then listen to one more girly rhyme

But these flowers have still survived

Long enough for me to gather them up

And present them before your eyes

These poems are truths I've gathered

In my garden and fields of thousands

I've gathered them with an eye for beauty and pain and

all the things life lets you gain

These poems I've offered to you because they are what I

feel is true

And if I never presented them then surely I would live

life tormented

Knowing I let wither such beautiful flowers